Shark vs. Penguin

Revised Edition

Mary Meinking

CAPSTONE PRESS
a capstone imprint

www.capstonepub.com
Visit our website to find out
more information about
Heinemann-Raintree books.

To order:
☎ Phone 800-747-4992
🖥 Visit www.capstonepub.com
to browse our catalog and order online.

© 2011 Heinemann Library
an imprint of Capstone Global Library, LLC
Chicago, Illinois

Edited by Rebecca Rissman, Dan Nunn,
    and Catherine Veitch
Designed by Joanna Hinton Malivoire
Levelling by Jeanne Clidas
Picture research by Hannah Taylor
Production by Victoria Fitzgerald
Originated by Capstone Global Library

**Library of Congress Cataloging-in-Publication
Data**
Meinking, Mary.
  Shark vs. penguin / Mary Meinking.
    p. cm.—(Predator vs. prey)
  title: Shark versus penguin
  Includes bibliographical references and index.
  ISBN 978-1-4109-9816-3 (paperback)
1. Sharks—Food—Juvenile literature. 2. Penguins—
Defenses—Juvenile literature. 3. Penguins—Preditors
of—Juvenile literature. 4. Predation (Biology)—Juvenile
literature. I. Title. II. Title: Shark versus penguin.
  QL638.9.M5226 2011
    598.47'147—dc22   2010016927

Acknowledgments
We would like to thank the following for permission
to reproduce photographs: agefotostock: Animals
Animals/James Watt, 17, Kelvin Aitken, 27, WaterFrame/
Reinhard Dirscherl, 23; Alamy: AfriPics.com, 10, 24,
25, David Fleetham, 4, Keren Su/China Span, 28, KIKE
CALVO, 29, Nigel Hicks, cover bottom; Ardea Picture
Library: Valerie Taylor, 8; FLPA: Minden Pictures/Fred
Bavendam, 12, Minden Pictures/Mike Parry, cover
top, 9, Minden Pictures/Stephen Belcher, 15, 19;
Getty Images: Kevin Schafer, 11, Martin Harvey, 14;
iStockphoto: Dr Awie Badenhorst, 5, Leicafoto, 6, Werner
Janse van Rensburg, 7; Nature Picture Library: Tom
Walmsley, 26; Newscom: Hawaii DLNR/MEG/GWGLA,
13, imageBROKER/Ingo Schulz, 18; Shutterstock: Anna
Phillips, 22, Brandy McKnight, 16, Nicole Beutell, 21,
stefbennett, 20

We would like to thank Michael Bright for his invaluable
help in the preparation of this book.

Every effort has been made to contact copyright holders
of any material reproduced in this book. Any omissions
will be rectified in subsequent printings if notice is given
to the publisher.

All the Internet addresses (URLs) given in this book were
valid at the time of going to press. However, due to the
dynamic nature of the Internet, some addresses may
have changed, or sites may have changed or ceased to
exist since publication. While the author and publisher
regret any inconvenience this may cause readers, no
responsibility for any such changes can be accepted by
either the author or the publisher.

Some words are shown in bold, **like this.** You can find
out what they mean by looking in the glossary.

Contents

Going Teeth to Beak

Jaws snap! Flippers splash! Two animals battle in the deep blue sea. Here's the world's most dangerous fish, the great white shark. It's up against a waddling challenger, the penguin.

shark

penguin

5

These animals live along Africa's coastline. Both have strengths that will help them in this battle.

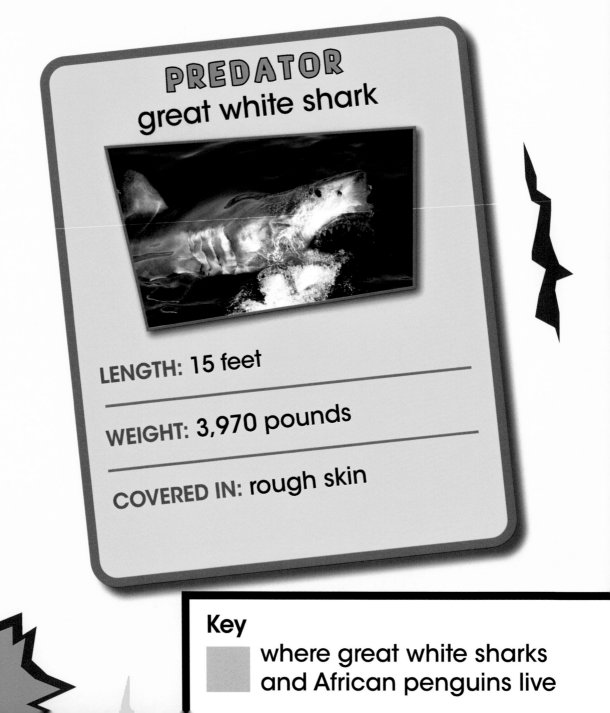

PREDATOR
great white shark

LENGTH: 15 feet

WEIGHT: 3,970 pounds

COVERED IN: rough skin

Key

where great white sharks and African penguins live

PREY
African penguin

LENGTH: 2 feet

WEIGHT: 7 pounds

COVERED IN: short, stiff feathers

Africa

Hunting Machine

The shark zooms through the water after its **prey**. It is pointed on both ends like an airplane. It steers with its two wing-like **pectoral** fins.

pectoral fin

Did You Know?

Great whites have rows of saw-like teeth. When a tooth falls out a new one moves into its place. They will have 3,000 teeth during their life.

Water Wings

The penguin is a bird but it can't fly. Instead it soars through the water. The penguin's wings are paddle-like flippers.

Did You Know?

African penguins are also called jackass penguins because they sound like donkeys. Hee-haw!

Who's Hungry?

The shark is a **carnivore,** or an animal that eats other animals. Sometimes the shark bumps into **prey** before it eats it. Special **cells** on its snout tell how things taste by how they feel.

Did You Know?

Sharks eat almost anything! Great whites eat fish, seals, turtles, and even whales. Some have even eaten cans, license plates, and surfboards.

surfboard

Sneak Attack

The penguin slides into the sea. It swims with its group and hunts for fish. The shark feels the **vibration**, or movement, of the penguins in the water. The shark moves towards them.

15

The penguin is **camouflaged**. Fish swimming under the penguin can't see its white belly that **blends** into the sky. Fish above the penguin can't see its black back that blends in with the dark sea bottom.

The shark smells or tastes the water as it searches for food.

The shark swims under the penguins, looking for one that is alone. The shark finds one! Its powerful tail pushes it through the water. The shark's eyes roll back just as it slams into the penguin. They both shoot into the air!

They come splashing down. The startled penguin swims away from the shark. Its flippers flap two times every second to shoot through the water. But the giant shark is on its tail!

Did You Know?

African penguins can swim at 15 miles per hour. That's three times faster than Olympic champions swim. But great whites can swim at 35 miles per hour!

The penguin uses its tail and feet to turn quickly. It **zigzags**, or swims in a Z-shaped pattern. It's trying to lose the shark. The shark stays with the penguin. It uses its **pectoral** fins to turn. But the shark can't turn as sharply as the penguin.

penguin's foot

The penguin picks up speed. It **porpoises,** or shoots into the air. It grabs a quick breath before splashing back into the water. The penguin porpoises toward the shore. This keeps it ahead of the shark. The penguin shoots onto the beach.

And the Winner Is...

...the penguin! It was lucky this time. But it had better stick with its group next time. Being an **agile** swimmer saved its life. The shark is big and not as flexible as the penguin.

What Are the Odds?

A great white shark catches its **prey** about once every two tries! It has to surprise its prey instead of trying to out-swim it. A great white can eat 24 pounds of meat in a single bite!

Glossary

agile quick and flexible

blend when things look so alike that you cannot tell them apart

camouflage animal's covering that helps it blend in with its surroundings

carnivore animal that eats meat

cell smallest part of a living thing

pectoral pair of fins behind a fish's head that helps them turn

porpoise leap out of the water and dive back in while speeding forward

predator animal that hunts other animals

prey animal that is hunted by other animals for food

vibration shaking back and forth motion

zigzag several sharp turns to change direction

Find Out More

Books

Ganeri, Anita. *Animal Top Tens: The Oceans' Most Amazing Animals.* Chicago: Raintree, 2008.

Spilsbury, Richard. *Animals under Threat: Great White Shark.* Chicago: Heinemann Library, 2004.

Webb, Sophie. *My Season with Penguins: An Antarctic Journal.* New York: Sandpiper, 2004.

Websites

http://kids.nationalgeographic.com/ Animals/CreatureFeature/Great-white-shark
Visit this Website to learn more about great white sharks.

http://www.antarcticconnection.com/ antarctic/wildlife/penguins/index.shtml
Find out more about different types of penguin on this Website.

http://www.oceansforyouth.org/kidscorner. html
Go to this Website to find out more about animals that live in the oceans.

Index